gardening
& planting
by the
mo🌕n
2020

nick kollerstrom

foulsham
LONDON • NEW YORK • TORONTO • SYDNEY

foulsham

An imprint of Foulsham Publishing Ltd

The Old Barrel Store, Drayman's Lane, Marlow, Bucks SL7 2FF

Foulsham books can be found in all good bookshops and direct from www.foulsham.com

Dedicated to the memory of Frau Maria Thun, pioneer of lunar gardening

ISBN: 978-0-572-04795-5

Copyright © 2019 Nick Kollerstrom

Cover photograph © Garden Picture Library

Series, format and layout design © 2019 Foulsham Publishing Ltd

The moral right of the author has been asserted

A CIP record for this book is available from the British Library

Typeset in India by Lapiz Digital Services, Chennai

Printed and bound by CPI Group (UK) Ltd, Croydon, CR0 4YY

Contents

The pull of the Moon is considerable. Not only does it move twice a day, it pulls on the Earth. Many gardeners and farmers are rediscovering the benefit of planting according to its phases, part of a profound knowledge neglected by modern techniques.

Harmony, A New Way of Looking at our World, by HRH The Prince of Wales, with Tony Juniper and Ian Skelly, 2010, p.137.

Introduction

To everything there is a season and a time to every purpose under heaven; a time to be born and a time to die: a time to plant, and a time to pluck up what is planted...

Ecclesiastes 3: 1–2

 here is no denying that alongside our high-speed, high-tech twenty-first century life there exists an ever-growing focus on eating well and on growing our own produce for personal consumption as a means of improving both our own health and the well-being of the planet. If we are going to invest our time and energy in this way, of course, we want the results to be as successful as possible. Decades ago, while studying the philosophy of Rudolf Steiner and working on a bio-dynamic farm inspired by his indications, I was startled to discover that lunar rhythms in planting really work. My first lunar calendar was produced in 1980 with my colleague Simon Best. To our delight, our gardening trials kept getting the results!

Steiner had explained how there were four basic formative forces that worked in Nature, and these are, of course, related to the four traditional elements. Gradually, over the years, his followers developed the notion of cosmic-etheric forces related to the Moon's passage through the Zodiac.

Our calendar uses the correct zodiac as it has existed in unchanging splendour for 2,500 years, consisting of twelve equal thirty-degree divisions of the sky. We acknowledge the profound effect of the lunar phases upon growth and fertility and, in accordance with tradition, our calendar uses the positions of the two most important planets, Saturn and Venus as well as the rising and setting of the Moon each day, as research has shown that organisms respond to Moonrise.

In today's world, many people do not even know the length of a lunar month. Even straightforward information about the lunar effect on the female menstrual cycle is still basically taboo. As far as I know, all living things respond to the lunar month in their fertility and growth, but somehow modern attitudes are sceptical of this. I have no doubt that if more people were open-minded enough to attune with the changing Moon, we would enjoy a more gentle and peaceful world.

Regular readers will notice that this edition is in a new format. This is in response to the feedback we have received. You tell us you don't need so much of the theory, it's the annual calendar that you really value. We value every comment we receive, and so we hope this new edition will please. For another year, we wish you the best of success in your garden.

The Four Elements

Clear the sheds of dung, but not at new moon or half moon.

Cato, *On Farming*

lthough modern lunar gardening guides tend to disagree on many issues, they do concur on one point: they all use a notion of dividing the zodiac into four periods, each connected with a particular element – Earth, Air, Fire and Water. At the core of this calendar is a four-element pattern, generated by the motion of the Moon against the stars, a modern system, based on an ancient idea.

Each month, the Moon moves around the sky against the 12 constellations of the zodiac, each of which has its particular affinity with one of the four elements. Each of the elements has three constellations linked to it, spaced equally around the circle of the zodiac. The diagram below shows the sky-triangles, or trigons, that map the three related signs. The 27-day orbit of the Moon against the stars means that each element lasts for two or three days and is repeated every nine days. The elements of Earth, Water, Air and Fire are said to influence the growth and performance of a particular sort of plant, respectively Root, Leaf, Flower and Fruit-seed. Further division into the well-known 12 signs of the zodiac is secondary in this scheme.

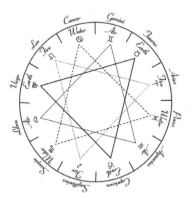

The four-element cycle underlying the zodiac

The theory is that in nature there are four kinds of subtle energy, 'formative forces', which work to influence the way a plant will develop, linking the time of sowing to the final condition of the crop when harvested. These forces are activated by the Moon's passage through the zodiac-elements, as the seed is sown.

The Star Rhythm

The sequence of element days, the star rhythm, runs: Root days, Flower days, Leaf days and then Fruit-seed days.

Root days are the times to sow carrots, potatoes, radishes and other root crops. These days occur when the Moon passes in front of the stars of one of three planets linked to the Earth element: Taurus, Virgo and Capricorn. When this happens, the Moon is said to have an Earth-type energy. If the weather is unsuitable for sowing those particular crops, simply wait for the next set of Root days nine days later.

Root days relate to the Earth signs   *Taurus*   *Virgo*   *Capricorn*

Leaf days are times when the Moon is in front of the constellations related to Water – Cancer, Scorpio and Pisces – and is the time to sow lettuce, cabbage and other leafy crops.

Leaf days relate to the Water signs   *Cancer*   *Scorpio*   *Pisces*

Flower days relate to the Air signs – Gemini, Libra and Aquarius – and are the best times to sow broccoli, globe artichoke, cauliflowers and similar plants.

Flower days relate to the Air signs   *Gemini*   *Libra*   *Aquarius*

Fruit-seed days relate to the Fire signs – Aries, Leo and Sagittarius – and are ideal for sowing tomatoes, beans and peas.

Fruit-seed days relate to the Fire signs   *Aries*   *Leo*   *Sagittarius*

Belief in the Moon's influence on the fertility of plants was once firmly embedded in the consciousness of ancient people and, as this is rediscovered scientifically today, farmers are again coming to regard the application of lunar cycles as a valuable practice.

Gardening Aspects

To the better furthering of the gardener's travails, he ought afore to consider, that the Garden earth be apt and good, wel turned in with dung, at a due time of the year, in the increase of the Moon, she occupying an apt place in the Zodiack, in agreeable aspect of Saturn, and well-placed in the sight of heaven ... for otherwise his care and pains bestowed about the seeds and plants, nothing availeth the Garden.

Thomas Hill, *The Gardener's Labyrinth*, 1577

s viewed from the Earth at Full Moon, the Sun and the Moon are said to be in opposition. Two weeks later at New Moon they form the aspect called conjunction. An aspect is an angle, measured around the ecliptic from the centre of the Earth, expressing a symmetry within the zodiac. In order of decreasing strength, the aspects are:

☌ conjunction (0°)   ☉ solar eclipse (0°)

☍ opposition (180°)   ☽ lunar eclipse (180°)

△ trine (120°)

□ square (90°)

✳ sextile (60°)

The square and opposition are considered inhibiting and stressful, whereas the trine and the sextile are thought to be beneficial and harmonious.

Each month, the Moon forms similar angles or aspects with Saturn and with the other planets. The Moon–Saturn relationship seems to have particular importance to agriculture and the life of plants. Our calendar indicates most of the Moon–Saturn aspects as they occur, some Moon–Sun aspects when they are relevant, and all the aspects between Moon and Venus as they fall on Flower days. The Venus aspects are recommended for working with flowers – sowing, planting out and grafting. In his ever-popular *Herbal*, Culpeper gave advice about when to pick herbs in terms of finding the right celestial aspects:

'*Let them be full ripe when they are gathered, and forget not the celestial harmony before mentioned; for I have found from experience that their virtues are twice as great at such times as others.*'

How to Use the Lunar Calendar

When you cut down elm, pine, walnut and all other timber, cut it when the Moon is waning, in the afternoon, and not under a south wind.

Cato, *On Farming*

his calendar is designed as a practical tool for the gardener and farmer, containing the key information needed on the two monthly cycles for which there is substantial evidence of their effects on gardening: the waxing and waning Moon, and the sidereal 27-day cycle. It also includes other, less well documented but potentially important information about aspects.

Readers may wish to do their own research, sowing some of their crop at an optimal time and more at a negative time to see whether there is any difference in the results. Ideally, a proper experiment requires at least a dozen rows, with equal amounts of seed sown per row on different days, and all harvested in rotation after the same length of time. Over time, one can distinguish lunar patterns from effects created by weather or other influences.

It is not always easy to co-ordinate a gardening schedule to the Moon – we all seem to be so busy these days – but with a little planning it can be achieved, hopefully with a positive effect. Of course, there will always have to be an element of judgement and compromise. For maximum yield, one aims to sow seeds at the peak times of the relevant sidereal energy cycle, yet there is no point in doing so if the ground is too wet, too dry or too cold. Use the following information as a starting point to help you tap into the cosmic influences and improve your crops.

Identifying Your Crops

All plants can be divided into one of four groups, each related to one of the four elements: Earth, Water, Air and Fire.

EARTH
ROOT PLANTS

Asparagus	Horseradish	Onion	Spring onion
Beetroot (red beet)	Jerusalem artichoke	Parsnip	(scallion)
Carrot	Leek	Potato	Swede
Garlic	Mushroom	Radish	Turnip

WATER
LEAF PLANTS

Asparagus	Celery	Fennel	Rhubarb
Basil	Chicory (Belgian	Lettuce	Sage
Bay	endive)	Mint	Sorrel
Brussels sprout	Coriander	Mustard and cress	Spinach
Cabbage	Cress	Parsley	Thyme

AIR
FLOWERING PLANTS

Artichoke	Broccoli	Elderflower
Borage	Cauliflower	Flowering plants

FIRE
FRUIT-SEED PLANTS

Apple	Broad bean	French bean	Plum
Apricot	Cherry	Gooseberry	Pumpkin
Asparagus pea	Courgette	Marrow	Runner bean
Aubergine	(zucchini)	Nectarine	Sweetcorn (corn)
(eggplant)	Cucumber	Pea	Tomato
Blackberry	Fig	Pear	Vine

When to Sow, Cultivate and Harvest

For sowing crops, observe the four-element cycle. In the calendar, these are shown as Root, Leaf, Flower and Fruit-seed days. Use the lists above to identify the day on which your crop should be sown.

If convenient, sowings are best made on the day nearest to the middle of any of the three Moon signs of the appropriate element. Prepare the soil on the same day. Avoid sowing just before the Moon moves out of a sign. Such transition times are given to the nearest hour. In Australia, one of the fathers of bio-dynamics, Alex Podolinsky, advocates sowing just as the Moon enters a new Moon-sign element, so the seed has a full two days in that quality before it changes, on the grounds that it takes that long to germinate. That view may be important in drought-prone countries.

Bio-dynamic farmers believe that any disturbance of the soil should be carried out in the same Moon-sign element in which the seed was sown. Lettuce, for example, is sown on a Leaf day, so its soil preparation as well as subsequent thinning out, weeding and so on should also be done on a Leaf day to enhance the effect.

Both experiments and experience seem to suggest that harvesting as well as sowing should be done on the relevant element days, when the weather permits. For root crops to be stored over winter, harvest on a Root day nearest to the New Moon. Fortunately, there is no hurry in harvesting root crops, so you can usually select an optimum time.

Using the Star Rhythm

If, for practical reasons, you cannot sow at the optimum times, at least try to avoid the worst times. The following diagram shows the regular wave pattern followed by the cycle of the four elements.

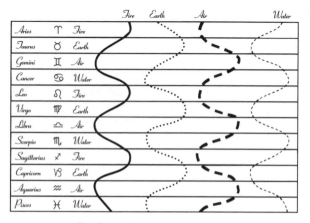

The four-element energy cycles

Root crops, for example, should ideally be sown during Earth days for optimal yield, but if this is impossible, try to avoid planting on days at the trough in the cycle when the Moon is in the opposite element, in this case Water days. The same principle applies to other elements.

The Best Times to Plant — Moonrise and Moonset

Gardeners are familiar with the idea that the time of day at which certain operations are performed is important. As the celestial element defines the best day for planting, Moonrise or Moonset suggests the best time of day to do the work. The calendar therefore indicates the time of Moonrise and Moonset each day, an hour either side being recommended as the best time to undertake any planting, working or gardening linked to the particular element of the day. Moonrise occurs in the daytime during the waxing phase, so this time is given for these dates. In the waning phase, Moonset occurs during the day, so this time is given. Thus Moonrise just before Full Moon happens in late afternoon. On the day of Full Moon, the Moon rises as the Sun sets.

Moonrise times are given for zero degrees longitude. For any other longitude, obtain the time of rising by adding one hour per 15 degrees of longitude due west. If your position is three degrees due west, for example, add 12 minutes to the times given in the calendar. Also the Moon rises earlier due north. Readers in other latitudes can check this by watching the Moon rise and comparing the time of day to that given here.

Moonrise and Moonset are especially significant if a relevant aspect is being formed by the Moon that day, for example with the Sun or Saturn.

Laboratory research by US biologist Frank Brown has demonstrated that the greatest metabolic rate in both plants and small animals was registered at the times of Moonrise and culmination, when it reaches its highest point in the sky about six hours later. US traditions take these as the best times of day for fishing.

For effective lunar planting, seed should really begin to germinate as soon as it is sown by beginning to absorb moisture from the soil; so it is preferable, at least in warm weather, to sow seeds in the afternoon when the soil will remain moist for longer after sowing.

Planting out crops is, in general, best done in the evening so they have the night to settle in and rest, while pruning is best done in the morning so that the Sun will dry up the cut surface, thereby inhibiting bleeding. Traditionally, crops were harvested in the morning.

Grafting is generally a spring activity and pruning is one for late autumn and winter.

It is also recommended that pruning should be done on the waning Moon and grafting on the waxing Moon. Planting out should be done in the waxing Moon, if possible in the same element in which the sowings were made.

The Harmony of a Sun–Moon Trine

The calendar gives the trine (120°) angle between Sun and Moon, as happens twice a month. This is a harmonious aspect free of stress or conflict. Its moment of linking the two luminaries is a good time for many things. Like the event of Moonrise, it seems never before to have featured in a UK lunar-gardening guide: the idea came from the American book *Gardening Success with Lunar Aspects* by Adèle Barger (1976). This aspect is of particular interest for crops ruled by the Sun, for example oranges or vines.

Growing Flowers

For Flower days, the aspects between the Moon and Venus are given. A Moon–Venus energy is ideal for sowing or planting flowers, especially roses, which are ruled by Venus. The square aspects are also included, even though some might view them as unsuitable, expressing difficulty and stress. Alternatively, they could be viewed as assisting the development of structure, so it is up to you to choose.

Trees and Perennials

When working with trees or woody plants, choose a Saturn aspect for the most propitious time. The calendar gives three types of Moon–Saturn aspect each month: the opposition (180°), the trine (120°) and the sextile (60°). Growers should be mainly concerned with the Saturn aspects on Fruit-seed days, as most of their trees will be fruit-bearing. Because trees are going to last for years, there is all the more reason to identify the optimal date for planting. There may be a choice here: if planting a honeysuckle or clematis to grow up a wall, choose a Flower day, then look for either a Saturn aspect for durability or a Venus aspect for pretty flowers.

How to Read the Calendar

Each page is devoted to a single week, and each day provides all the essential information to help you make the most of your lunar gardening, indicated by various symbols. Each piece of information will be found in the same position on the daily calendars so they will soon become familiar. The calendar gives practical notes for the days to help your understanding of the aspects given, and makes suggestions on gardening activities. The notes also give the sacred Moons, such as when Easter falls or the Jewish New Year begins. Notice that the Muslim months begin a day or two after the actual New Moon, and these beginning days should be when you can first see the thin crescent of the New Moon at dusk. There's also space to record your own gardening notes.

The following symbols are used on the calendar. The key is repeated throughout the calendar along the bottom of the pages for easy reference.

Elements
These indicate the type of crop to sow on the relevant days.

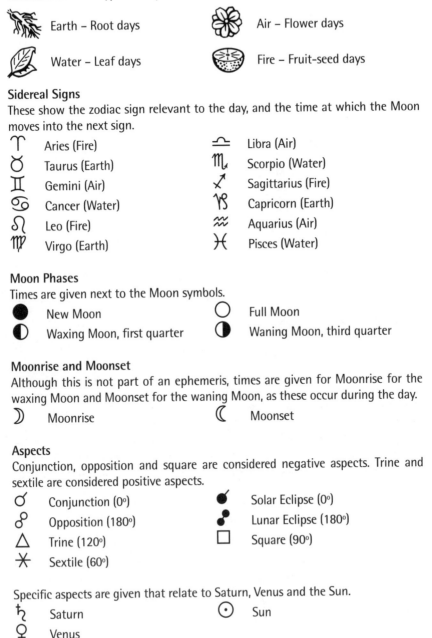

Earth – Root days

Air – Flower days

Water – Leaf days

Fire – Fruit-seed days

Sidereal Signs
These show the zodiac sign relevant to the day, and the time at which the Moon moves into the next sign.

♈ Aries (Fire)

♎ Libra (Air)

♉ Taurus (Earth)

♏ Scorpio (Water)

♊ Gemini (Air)

♐ Sagittarius (Fire)

♋ Cancer (Water)

♑ Capricorn (Earth)

♌ Leo (Fire)

♒ Aquarius (Air)

♍ Virgo (Earth)

♓ Pisces (Water)

Moon Phases
Times are given next to the Moon symbols.

● New Moon

○ Full Moon

◐ Waxing Moon, first quarter

◑ Waning Moon, third quarter

Moonrise and Moonset
Although this is not part of an ephemeris, times are given for Moonrise for the waxing Moon and Moonset for the waning Moon, as these occur during the day.

☽ Moonrise

☾ Moonset

Aspects
Conjunction, opposition and square are considered negative aspects. Trine and sextile are considered positive aspects.

♂ Conjunction (0º)

Solar Eclipse (0º)

♄ Opposition (180º)

Lunar Eclipse (180º)

△ Trine (120º)

☐ Square (90º)

✳ Sextile (60º)

Specific aspects are given that relate to Saturn, Venus and the Sun.

♄ Saturn

☉ Sun

♀ Venus

Nodes

These are the points at which the Moon crosses the ecliptic.

☊ North node   ☋ South node

Apogee and Perigee

The apogee is the time at which the Moon is furthest from the Earth in its orbit, the perigee is when it is closest to the Earth.

𝒜 Apogee   𝒫 Perigee

Understanding the Entries

Here are a couple of examples, showing how to read the daily entries.

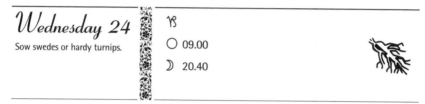

Wednesday 24

Sow swedes or hardy turnips.

♑

○ 09.00

☽ 20.40

This is a Root day because the Moon is in Capricorn, an Earth constellation, shown by the zodiacal glyph on the left. The Moon-quarter symbol indicates that this is a Full Moon, its time to the nearest hour noted next to the symbol. The time of Moonrise, to the nearest ten minutes, is given next to the crescent.

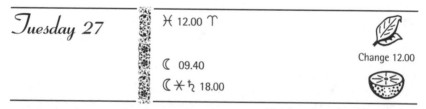

Tuesday 27

♓ 12.00 ♈

☾ 09.40

☾ ⚹ ♄ 18.00

Change 12.00

The transition from one zodiac sign to another, the ingress, occurs at noon. As the Moon progresses through the zodiac, so the ruling elements shift according to the same timetable, so the morning is Pisces, a Water sign giving a Leaf day, while the afternoon is Aries, a Fire sign, giving a Fruit-seed day. Moonset is at 09.40, then in the afternoon there is a Moon-Saturn sextile (60°) aspect, which is good for trees.

Checklist for Using the Calendar

Annual crops

Follow the four-element rhythms, sowing as near to the centre of the relevant sign as is convenient. The same element-sign (Root, Leaf, Flower, Fruit-seed) reappears every nine days, so if you miss the appropriate period the next may still be convenient.

Grafting and transplanting
Try to do this kind of activity under a waxing Moon.

Harvesting
Fruits picked at New Moon will store better, whereas fruits to be eaten fresh are best picked at Full Moon. Crops should be harvested in the same Moon-sign element in which they were sown if you wish to obtain seeds for next year's crop.

Perennial crops, shrubs or trees
Try to take advantage of a Saturn–Moon aspect when planting. If a tree or bush is fruit-bearing, you can also try to plant or graft it on a Fruit-seed day.

Pruning and gelding
The lunar water uptake cycle is relevant here and near Full Moon is not recommended for pruning; try to time such activity for the waning Moon.

Sowing times
Sow and plant as close to the hour of Moonrise as possible, with adjustments to your longitude and latitude. Avoid sowing for a few hours either side of the nodes, the perigee or an eclipse. Where drought is a problem, note that seeds tend to absorb the greatest amount of water on the days prior to the Full Moon, so sowing at this time should lead to optimal germination.

Times and Time Zones

All times are given in the 24-hour clock. Aspect times are given to the nearest ten minutes, Moonrise and Moonset times to the nearest ten minutes and other times to the nearest hour.

All times are GMT, or British Summer Time (BST, 1 hour added). Users in other parts of the world will need to adjust the times according to their time zone, adding or subtracting the number of hours given below.

Time Zone Adjustments for North America		Time Zone Adjustments for Australasia	
Atlantic	-4 hours	New Zealand	+12 hours
Eastern	-5 hours	Western Australia	+ 8 hours
Central	-6 hours	Southern Australia	+ 9½ hours
Mountain	-7 hours	Northern Territory	+ 9½ hours
Pacific	-8 hours	New South Wales	+ 10 hours
Yukon	-9 hours	Victoria	+ 10 hours
Alaska-Hawaii	-10 hours	Queensland	+ 10 hours
Bering	-11 hours	Tasmania	+ 10 hours

October 2019

Tuesday 1	♎	☽ ⚹ ♄ 09.40	
	☽ 10.40		

Wednesday 2 Sow varieties of lettuce around noon for over-wintering under cloches.	♎ 03.00 ♏ ☽ 12.00		

Thursday 3	♏ ☽ 13.10	☽ ⚹ ☉ 05.40	

Friday 4	♏ 08.00 ♐ ☽ 14.10	☽ ⚹ ♀ 08.30	Change 08.00

Saturday 5	♐ ◑ ☽ 15.00	♉ 20.00	AM only

Sunday 6 Harvest Festival	♐ 17.00 ♑ ☽ 15.40		Change 17.00

♎ Libra *Air*	♏ Scorpio *Water*	♐ Sagittarius *Fire*	♑ Capricorn *Earth*	♒ Aquarius *Air*	♓ Pisces *Water*

October 2019

Monday 7

♑

☽ 16.10

Tuesday 8

♑

☽△☉ 10.20

☽ 16.40

Wednesday 9

♑ 05.00 ♒

☽△♀ 19.50

☽ 17.00

Change 05.00

Thursday 10

Prepare new rose beds for planting, or plant lily-of-the-valley. Plant out herbaceous perennials.

♒

☽ 17.10

𝒜 19.00

Friday 11

♒ 18.00 ♓

☽ 17.30

Change 18.00

Saturday 12

♓

☽ 17.50

Sunday 13

This was known as the Hunter's Moon in times gone by.

♓

○ 22.00

☽ 18.00

| ♀ Venus | ☉ Sun | △ Trine | ♂ Conjunction | ◖ Solar eclipse |
| ♄ Saturn | ☐ Square | ✳ Sextile | ☍ Opposition | ☋ Lunar eclipse |

October 2019

Monday 14	♓ 06.00 ♈ ☾ 07.50		Change 06.00
Tuesday 15 Prune and tend to trees today.	♈ ☾ 09.00	☾ ☍ ♀ 09.30	
Wednesday 16	♈ 16.00 ♉ ☾ 10.10		Change 16.00
Thursday 17 The Sun passes by Spica today, the benevolent star of the grain harvest.	♉ ☾ 11.20		
Friday 18	♉ ☾ 12.30		
Saturday 19	♉ 01.00 ♊ ☾ 13.30		
Sunday 20	♊ ☾ 14.20	☊ 08.00 ☾ △ ♀ 14.30	PM only

October 2019

Monday 21

♊ 07.00 ♋
◗
☾ 15.00

Change 07.00

Tuesday 22

Take cuttings of bay and rue. Divide roots of mint to re-plant elsewhere.

♋
☾ 15.30

Wednesday 23

♋ 11.00 ♌
☾ 16.00

Change 11.00

Thursday 24

Pick late tomatoes and let them ripen on trays. Work on any fruit trees, especially around 4-5 pm.

♌
☾ 16.20

Friday 25

♌ 12.00 ♍
☾✶♀ 06.00
☾ 16.40

AM

PM

Saturday 26

♍
☾ 17.00
℘ 12.00

No Planting

✕

Sunday 27

The Indian festival of *Diwali* begins. Wish your family Shubh *Diwali* and light candles. End of British Summer Time: clocks go back one hour.

♍ 11.00 ♎
☾ 16.30

Change 11.00

♈	♉	♊	♋	♌	♍
Aries	Taurus	Gemini	Cancer	Leo	Virgo
Fire	*Earth*	*Air*	*Water*	*Fire*	*Earth*

October/November 2019

Monday 28
Cut out the fruited blackberry and loganberry canes and train in new roots.

♎

● 04.00

☽ 07.00

Tuesday 29
Harvest herbs for drying and storage over winter in the afternoon.

♎ 12.00 ♏

☽ ☌ ♀ 15.10

☽ 08.30

AM

PM

Wednesday 30
Start planting winter lettuce around 10 am and force-grow rhubarb in a warm greenhouse.

♏

☽ 09.50

Thursday 31
Samhain, a gathering of the clans before winter. Halloween, traditionally a time of other-worldly interference in human affairs. *Diwali* ends.

♏ 16.00 ♐

☽ 10.50

Change 16.00

Friday 1
All Saints' Day

♐

☽ ⚹ ☉ 19.20

☊ 22.00

☽ 11.50

AM only

Saturday 2

♐ 24.00 ♑

☽ ☌ ♄ 07.30

☽ 12.40

Sunday 3
Compost the leaves you rake up in the garden.

♑

☽ ⚹ ♀ 15.40

☽ 13.10

♎	♏	♐	♑	♒	♓
Libra	Scorpio	Sagittarius	Capricorn	Aquarius	Pisces
Air	*Water*	*Fire*	*Earth*	*Air*	*Water*

November 2019

Monday 4

♑
◑
☽ 13.40

Tuesday 5

♑ 11.00 ♒
☽ 14.00

Change 11.00

Wednesday 6

♒
☽□♀ 10.40
☽ 14.20

Thursday 7

We are half-way between the Autumn Equinox and the Winter Solstice.

♒ 24.00 ♓
☽⚹♄ 07.20
☽ 14.40
A 09.00

Friday 8

Lift chicory and asparagus.

♓
☽ 14.50

Saturday 9

♓
☽△♀ 06.20
☽ 15.10

Sunday 10

♓ 12.00 ♈
☽ 15.30

AM

PM

| ♀ Venus | ⊙ Sun | △ Trine | ♂ Conjunction | ◐ Solar eclipse |
| ♄ Saturn | □ Square | ⚹ Sextile | ☍ Opposition | ☾ Lunar eclipse |

November 2019

Monday 11
Plant gooseberry bushes and raspberry canes, and sow round-seeded peas.

♈

☽ 15.50

Tuesday 12
Enjoy a night-time walk under the November Full Moon.

♈ 22.00 ♉

○ 14.00

☾ △ ♄ 06.40

Wednesday 13
Finish digging new beds and borders for winter weathering.

♉

☾ 08.10

Thursday 14
Turn over half-rotted compost, clear fallen leaves away from small plants so they are not too damp.

♉

☾ ☍ ♀ 14.20

☾ 09.20

Friday 15

♉ 06.00 ♊

☾ 10.20

Change 06.00

Saturday 16

♊

☊ 09.00

☾ 11.10

No Planting

X

Sunday 17

♊ 12.00 ♋

☾ △ ☉ 12.50

☾ 12.00

AM

PM

● New Moon   ◐ 1st quarter   ☽ Moonrise   ☊ North node   𝒜 Apogee
○ Full Moon   ◑ 3rd quarter   ☾ Moonset   ☋ South node   𝒫 Perigee

November 2019

Monday 18
♋

Pick herbs to dry. Take cuttings of bay and rue and place in pots of sand. Re-pot mint in the greenhouse.

☾ 12.30

Tuesday 19
♋ 16.00 ♌

◑

☾△♀ 12.00

☾ 13.00

Change 16.00

Wednesday 20
♌

Prune fruit-trees after planting. Stake trees.

☾ 13.20

Thursday 21
♌ 19.00 ♍

☾△♄ 06.40

☾ 13.40

Change 19.00

Friday 22
♍

☾ 14.10

Saturday 23
♍ 20.00 ♎

PM only

☾ 14.30

℘ 08.00

Sunday 24
♎

Prick out any perennials you have raised in the greenhouse and sow winter bedding plants.

☾ 14.50

♈	♉	♊	♋	♌	♍
Aries	Taurus	Gemini	Cancer	Leo	Virgo
Fire	*Earth*	*Air*	*Water*	*Fire*	*Earth*

November 2019

Monday 25

Cut back and tidy any flowering plants in the afternoon. In the greenhouse, start forcing bulbs and sow seed of most alpines. Finish planting roses.

♎ 22.00 ♏

☾ ✳ ♄ 11.00

☾ 15.20

Tuesday 26

♏

● 15.00

Wednesday 27

♏

☽ 08.30

Thursday 28

Sow melons for an early crop and early peas and dwarf beans for cropping under glass.

♏ 02.00 ♐

☽ ☌ ♀ 18.40

☽ 09.40

Friday 29

♐

PM only

☊ 04.00

☽ 10.30

Saturday 30

St Andrew's Day is celebrated in Scotland.

♐ 09.00 ♑

Change 09.00

☽ 11.10

♎	♏	♐	♑	♒	♓
Libra	Scorpio	Sagittarius	Capricorn	Aquarius	Pisces
Air	Water	Fire	Earth	Air	Water

December 2019

December Reminders —————————

Sunday 1
Advent Sunday; Christmas
decorations can go up now.

♑

☽ 11.40

☽ ⚹ ☉ 13.40

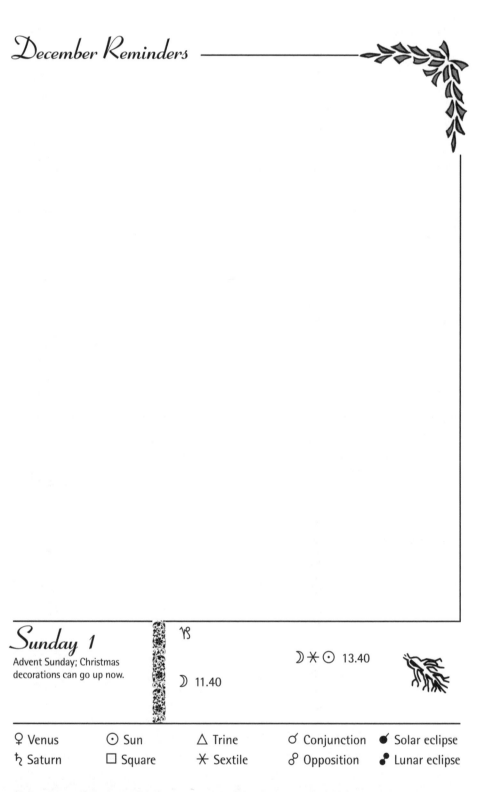

| ♀ Venus | ☉ Sun | △ Trine | ♂ Conjunction | ☀ Solar eclipse |
| ♄ Saturn | ☐ Square | ⚹ Sextile | ☍ Opposition | ☋ Lunar eclipse |

December 2019

Monday 2

♑ 19.00 ♒

☽ 12.00

Change 19.00

Tuesday 3

Work with flowering shrubs and trees around noon.

♒

☽ 12.20

Wednesday 4

♒

◐

☽ 12.40

Thursday 5

♒ 08.00 ♓

☽ 13.00

𝒜 04.00

Change 08.00

Friday 6

Another chance to re-pot mint in the greenhouse and take cuttings of bay and rue to place in pots of sand. St Nicholas's Day.

♓

☽ 13.20

Saturday 7

♓ 20.00 ♈

☽ 13.30

Change 20.00

Sunday 8

Sow melons around 1–2 pm for an early crop, and tomatoes for a summer crop in the greenhouse.

♈

☽ 13.50

● New Moon   ◑ 1st quarter   ☽ Moonrise   ☊ North node   𝒜 Apogee

○ Full Moon   ◐ 3rd quarter   ☾ Moonset   ☋ South node   𝑃 Perigee

December 2019

Monday 9
Work on vines or other fruits in the greenhouse in the afternoon.

♈

☽ 14.10

☽ △ ♀ 16.10
☽ △ ♄ 19.50

Tuesday 10

♈ 06.00 ♉

☽ 14.40

Change 06.00

Wednesday 11
Cover land with rotted-down compost.

♉

☽ 15.20

Thursday 12
Admire how high the Full Moon rises in the night sky.

♉ 13.00 ♊
○ 05.00
☾ 08.10

Change 13.00

Friday 13
Look for the multi-coloured Geminids meteor shower from a dark location after midnight. It's said to be the best shower of the year.

♊

☾ 09.10

☊ 14.00

No Planting

X

Saturday 14

♊ 18.00 ♋

☾ 10.00

☾ ☌ ♀ 16.00

Change 18.00

Sunday 15
Trim back lawn edges to make the garden tidy.

♋

☾ 10.30

♈	♉	♊	♋	♌	♍
Aries	Taurus	Gemini	Cancer	Leo	Virgo
Fire	Earth	Air	Water	Fire	Earth

December 2019

Monday 16
♋ 21.00 ♌

☾ 11.00

Tuesday 17
♌

☾ 11.30

Wednesday 18
♌

☾ △ ♄ 17.00

AM only

☾ 11.50

℘ 20.00

Thursday 19
Examine stored vegetables and remove any that are diseased.

♌ 00.00 ♍

◑

☾ △ ♀ 08.10

☾ 12.10

Friday 20
♍

☾ 12.30

Saturday 21
♍ 03.00 ♎

☾ ⚹ ☉ 11.50

☾ 12.50

☾ □ ♀ 15.50

Sunday 22
Winter solstice, the shortest day and longest night, when the Sun crosses over the Galactic Equator.

♎

☾ 13.20

♎	♏	♐	♑	♒	♓
Libra	Scorpio	Sagittarius	Capricorn	Aquarius	Pisces
Air	*Water*	*Fire*	*Earth*	*Air*	*Water*

December 2019

Monday 23	♎ 06.00 ♏︎ ☽ 13.50		Change 06.00
Tuesday 24	♏︎ ☽ 14.30		
Wednesday 25 Christmas Day and the twelve Holy nights begin.	♏︎ 11.00 ♐ ☽ 15.20		Change 11.00
Thursday 26 Solar eclipse on the Christmas New Moon.	♐ ● ☄ 05.00 ☽ 08.20	☊ 13.00	No Planting **X**
Friday 27 Clear vegetable plots and dispose of soft vegetable waste by digging it into trenches.	♐ 18.00 ♑ ☽ 09.00	☽ ♂ ♄ 12.10	Change 18.00
Saturday 28	♑ ☽ 09.40		
Sunday 29	♑ ☽ 10.10		

♀ Venus	☉ Sun	△ Trine	♂ Conjunction	● Solar eclipse
♄ Saturn	☐ Square	✳ Sextile	☍ Opposition	☄ Lunar eclipse

December 2019

Monday 30

♑ 04.00 ♒

☽ 10.30

Tuesday 31

New Year's Eve, 'Hogmanay' in Scotland. A fine flower day with a Sun – Moon sextile in the morning.

♒

☽✶☉ 10.30

☽ 10.50

Gardening Notes

January 2020

January Reminders

Wednesday 1
New Year's Day

♒ 16.00 ♓

☽ 11.00

☽ ⚹ ♄ 10.40

Change 16.00

Thursday 2

♓

☽ 11.20

♌ 02.00

Friday 3
Look for the meteor showers in the northeast sky after midnight.

♓

◐

☽ 11.40

☽ ⚹ ♀ 15.40

Saturday 4

♓ 05.00 ♈

☽ 11.50

Change 05.00

Sunday 5
Perihelion near 8 am, as the Earth reaches its nearest point to the Sun in midwinter. Twelfth Night, the last of the Holy Nights of Christmas.

♈

☽ 12.20

♈	♉	♊	♋	♌	♍
Aries	Taurus	Gemini	Cancer	Leo	Virgo
Fire	*Earth*	*Air*	*Water*	*Fire*	*Earth*

January 2020

Monday 6
Epiphany, when gifts of Gold, Frankincense and Myrrh were brought by the three Magi (astrologers) to the baby Jesus.

♈ 15.00 ♉

☽ △ ♄ 11.10

☽ 12.40

Change 15.00

Tuesday 7
♉

☽ 13.10

Wednesday 8
♉ 22.00 ♊

☽ 14.00

Thursday 9
♊

♌ 23.00

☽ 14.50

AM only

Friday 10
Partial lunar eclipse, keep out of the garden.

♊

○ ☊ 19.00

☽ 16.00

No Planting

X

Saturday 11
See how high the Full Moon rises in the midnight sky.

♊ 02.00 ♋

☾ 08.30

Sunday 12
♋

☾ 09.10

♎	♏	♐	♑	♒	♓
Libra	Scorpio	Sagittarius	Capricorn	Aquarius	Pisces
Air	Water	Fire	Earth	Air	Water

January 2020

Monday 13

♋ 04.00 ♌

☾ ☌ ♀ 13.40   AM only

☾ 09.30

♃ 20.00

Tuesday 14

Cut out any diseased or dead wood from fruit trees.

♌

☾ 10.00

Wednesday 15

A harmonious trine between the Sun and Moon.

♌ 06.00 ♍

☾ △ ☉ 06.40

☾ 10.20

Change 06.00

Thursday 16

♍

☾ 10.40

Friday 17

Mulch any empty ground with good compost.

♍ 08.00 ♎

◗

☾ 11.00

Change 08.00

Saturday 18

♎

☾ 11.20

Sunday 19

♎ 12.00 ♏

☾ ⚹ ♄ 11.20   AM

☾ 11.50   PM

♀ Venus   ☉ Sun   △ Trine   ☌ Conjunction   ◗ Solar eclipse

♄ Saturn   ☐ Square   ⚹ Sextile   ☍ Opposition   ☾ Lunar eclipse

January 2020

Monday 20
Time to sow early salad crops in the greenhouse, at the Moonset hour of noon if possible.

♏

☾ 12.30

Tuesday 21

♏ 18.00 ♐

☾ 13.10

Change 18.00

Wednesday 22

♐

☋ 21.00

AM only

☾ 14.10

Thursday 23
Sow fruit-crops in the greenhouse, using the Moonset hour of 3 pm.

♐

☾ 15.10

Friday 24

♐ 02.00 ♑

● 22.00

☾ 16.10

Saturday 25
Chinese New Year of the Metal Rat. Burns Night, *My love is like a red, red rose...* Enjoy some haggis to mark the occasion.

♑

☽ 08.10

Sunday 26

♑ 12.00 ♒

☽ 08.30

AM

PM

● New Moon   ◐ 1st quarter   ☽ Moonrise   ☊ North node   *A* Apogee

○ Full Moon   ◑ 3rd quarter   ☾ Moonset   ☋ South node   *P* Perigee

January 2020

Monday 27 ≈

☽ 08.50

Tuesday 28 ≈ 24.00 ♓

☽ ♂ ♀ 11.00

☽ 09.10

Wednesday 29 ♓

Sow salad crops in the
greenhouse or in plastic
cloches in a sheltered spot.

☽ 09.30

Thursday 30 ♓

Sow in the morning, with
harmonious Sun–Moon chime
at Moonrise hour.

☽ ✳ ☉ 07.50

☽ 09.40

Friday 31 ♓ 13.00 ♈

☽ 10.00

AM

PM

Gardening Notes

♈	♉	♊	♋	♌	♍
Aries	Taurus	Gemini	Cancer	Leo	Virgo
Fire	*Earth*	*Air*	*Water*	*Fire*	*Earth*

February 2020

February Reminders

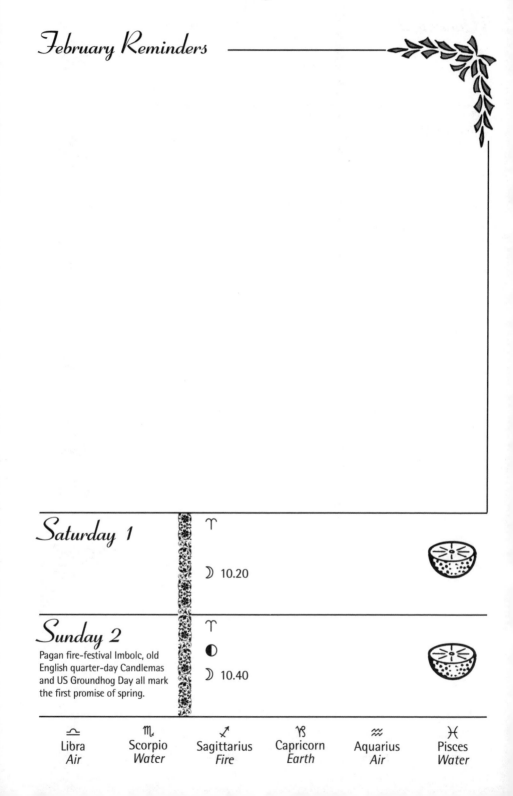

Saturday 1	♈		
	☽ 10.20		
Sunday 2 Pagan fire-festival Imbolc, old English quarter-day Candlemas and US Groundhog Day all mark the first promise of spring.	♈ ◐ ☽ 10.40		

♎	♏	♐	♑	♒	♓
Libra *Air*	Scorpio *Water*	Sagittarius *Fire*	Capricorn *Earth*	Aquarius *Air*	Pisces *Water*

February 2020

Monday 3

♈ 00.00 ♉

☽ 11.10

Tuesday 4
The half-way point between the winter solstice and spring equinox.

♉

☽ △ ☉ 16.20

☽ 11.50

Wednesday 5

♉ 08.00 ♊

☽ □ ♀ 14.20

☽ 12.30

Change 08.00

Thursday 6
Avoid the garden this morning under the north node.

♊

☊ 09.00

☽ 13.30

No Planting

X

Friday 7

♊ 13.00 ♋

☽ 14.40

AM

PM

Saturday 8
Clear dead material from leafy plants; sow salad crops under glass or in plastic cloches.

♋

☽ 16.10

Sunday 9
See how high this winter Full Moon rises.

♋ 14.00 ♌

○ 08.00

AM

PM

| ♀ Venus | ☉ Sun | △ Trine | ♂ Conjunction | ● Solar eclipse |
| ♄ Saturn | □ Square | ✳ Sextile | ♊ Opposition | ♠ Lunar eclipse |

February 2020

Monday 10
Tend to fruit trees only in the morning today.

Ω

$\mathbb{C}$ 08.00

P 20.00

AM only

Tuesday 11

Ω 14.00 ♍

$\mathbb{C} \triangle \hbar$ 17.40

$\mathbb{C}$ 08.20

AM

PM

Wednesday 12
Sow parsnips, garlic, carrots or radishes.

♍

$\mathbb{C} \, \theta \, \female$ 08.10

$\mathbb{C}$ 08.40

Thursday 13

♍ 15.00 ♎

$\mathbb{C} \triangle \odot$ 15.20

$\mathbb{C}$ 09.00

Change 15.00

Friday 14
St Valentine's Day. Sow early seeds for spring flowers.

♎

$\mathbb{C}$ 09.30

Saturday 15
Buddhist Nirvana day, when Buddha attained enlightenment.

♎ 18.00 ♏

$\mathbb{O}$

$\mathbb{C}$ 10.00

Change 18.00

Sunday 16

♏

$\mathbb{C}$ 10.30

● New Moon   ◐ 1st quarter   ☽ Moonrise Ω North node A Apogee

○ Full Moon   ◑ 3rd quarter $\mathbb{C}$ Moonset ∂ South node P Perigee

February 2020

Monday 17

♏ 24.00 ♐

☾ 11.10

Tuesday 18

Sow early peas and broad beans under cloches in a sheltered area, in the morning.

♐

☾ ✳ ☉ 09.00

☾ 12.00

Wednesday 19

♐

♉ (☊)

PM only

☾ 13.00

Thursday 20

Dig compost into the vegetable patch this afternoon.

♐ 08.00 ♑

☾ ☌ ♄ 14.20

☾ 14.00

Change 08.00

Friday 21

Sow root crops such as parsnips or beetroot.

♑

☾ 15.10

Saturday 22

♑ 19.00 ♒

☾ 16.20

Change 19.00

Sunday 23

♒

● 16.00

♈	♉	♊	♋	♌	♍
Aries	Taurus	Gemini	Cancer	Leo	Virgo
Fire	*Earth*	*Air*	*Water*	*Fire*	*Earth*

February 2020

Monday 24

☲

☽ 07.20

Tuesday 25

Throw a party to mark Mardi Gras, our Shrove Tuesday.

☲ 07.00 ♓

☽ ⚹ ♄ 14.10

☽ 07.30

Change 07.00

Wednesday 26

Ash Wednesday, Lent begins: renounce something, such as eggs or cheese to help the breeding farm animals.

♓

☽ 07.50

𝒜 12.00

Thursday 27

♓ 20.00 ♈

☽ ☌ ♀ 17.10

☽ 08.10

Change 20.00

Friday 28

♈

☽ 08.20

Saturday 29

♈

☽ 08.40

♎	♏	♐	♑	☲	♓
Libra	Scorpio	Sagittarius	Capricorn	Aquarius	Pisces
Air	*Water*	*Fire*	*Earth*	*Air*	*Water*

March 2020

March Reminders

Sunday 1

St David's Day, the feast day of the patron saint of Wales.

♈ 08.00 ♉

☽ 09.10

☽ △ ♄ 15.50

Change 08.00

♀ Venus	☉ Sun	△ Trine	♂ Conjunction	● Solar eclipse
♄ Saturn	□ Square	✳ Sextile	☍ Opposition	● Lunar eclipse

March 2020

Monday 2
Trim back and begin to water fuchsias and pelagonium roots to encourage them back to life.

♉
◑
☽ 09.40

Tuesday 3
♉ 18.00 ♊

☽ 10.20

Change 18.00

Wednesday 4
♊

☊ 15.00

☽ 11.10

No Planting

X

Thursday 5
Use the harmony of a Sun–Moon trine this morning, especially for flower crops.

♊ 23.00 ♋

☽ △ ☉ 07.50

☽ 12.20

Friday 6
♋

☽ 13.30

Saturday 7
♋

☽ 15.00

Sunday 8
See how things start to grow and germinate coming up to the Full Moon, especially if there has been some rain.

♋ 01.00 ♌

☽ △ ♀ 17.00

☽ 16.20

● New Moon ◐ 1st quarter ☽ Moonrise ☊ North node 𝒜 Apogee
○ Full Moon ◑ 3rd quarter ☾ Moonset ☋ South node 𝒫 Perigee

March 2020

Monday 9
A 'Supermoon' (near perigee).

♌
○ 18.00

Tuesday 10
The mating of farm animals will be more successful around the spring Full Moons.

♌ 01.00 ♍
☾ △ ♄ 08.30   PM only
☾ 06.40
℘ 07.00

Wednesday 11
Parsnips, garlic, carrots and radishes can be sown today.

♍
☾ 07.10

Thursday 12

♍ 00.00 ♎
☾ 07.30

Friday 13
Use the Moonset hour of 8 am to sow flowers.

♎
☾ 08.00

Saturday 14

♎ 01.00 ♏
☾ ✶ ♄ 10.10
☾ 08.30

Sunday 15
Start sowing salad crops and spinach, amd some early cabbage and Brussels sprouts.

♏
☾ 09.10

♈	♉	♊	♋	♌	♍
Aries	Taurus	Gemini	Cancer	Leo	Virgo
Fire	*Earth*	*Air*	*Water*	*Fire*	*Earth*

March 2020

Monday 16

♏ 06.00 ♐

◑

☾ 10.00

Change 06.00

Tuesday 17

St Patrick's Day; why not celebrate with a Guinness?

♐

☊ 01.00

☾ 10.50

☾ △ ♀ 17.30

PM only

Wednesday 18

♐ 14.00 ♑

☾ 12.00

AM

PM

Thursday 19

Sow new Jerusalem artichokes today, keeping them a good 30 cm apart, also parsnips, garlic, carrots and radishes.

♑

☾ 13.00

Friday 20

Spring Equinox. It's Nowruz, the Persian New Year.

♑

☾ 14.10

Saturday 21

♑ 01.00 ♒

☾ 15.20

Sunday 22

Mothering Sunday: visit the church where you were baptised or given Mum some flowers.

♒

☾ 16.30

♎	♏	♐	♑	♒	♓
Libra	Scorpio	Sagittarius	Capricorn	Aquarius	Pisces
Air	*Water*	*Fire*	*Earth*	*Air*	*Water*

March 2020

Monday 23
The Evening Star reaches its highest point tonight after sunset.

≈ 13.00 ♓

☾ 17.30

AM

PM

Tuesday 24
Hindu New Year

♓

● 09.00

♌ 15.00

Wednesday 25
Graft during the waxing Moon.

♓

☽ 06.10

Thursday 26
Plant late-flowering strawberries on suitable sites.

♓ 02.00 ♈

☽ 06.30

Friday 27

♈

☽ 06.50

Saturday 28

♈ 14.00 ♉

☽ ♂ ♀ 14.20

☽ 07.10

AM

PM

Sunday 29
British Summer Time begins, clocks go forward one hour.

♉

☽ 08.40

♀ Venus   ☉ Sun   △ Trine   ♂ Conjunction   ◖ Solar eclipse

♄ Saturn   □ Square   ✳ Sextile   ☍ Opposition   ◗ Lunar eclipse

March 2020

Monday 30

♉

☽ 09.20

Tuesday 31

♉ 02.00 ♊

♌ 18.00

AM only

☽ 10.10

Gardening Notes

April 2020

April Reminders

Wednesday 1	♊ ◑ ☽ 11.00	🌼

Thursday 2	♊ 09.00 ♋ ☽ ✶ ♀ 17.50 ☽ 12.10	🌼 Change 07.00 🍃

Friday 3
Use the Moonrise hour of 1–2 pm to sow leaf crop vegetables.

♋   ☽ 13.30   🍃

Saturday 4

♋ 13.00 ♌   ☽ 14.50   AM 🍃   PM 🍊

Sunday 5
Palm Sunday, which marks the start of Christian holy week.

♌   ☽ 16.20   🍊

♈ Aries Fire	♉ Taurus Earth	♊ Gemini Air	♋ Cancer Water	♌ Leo Fire	♍ Virgo Earth

April 2020

Monday 6

♌ 13.00 ♍

☽ 17.40

AM

PM

Tuesday 7

♍

☽ 19.10

ℙ 19.00

AM only

Wednesday 8
A 'Supermoon' (near perigee).

♍ 12.00 ♎

○ 04.00

☾ 06.30

AM

PM

Thursday 9
Maundy Thursday

♎

☾ 06.50

Friday 10
Good Friday

♎ 12.00 ♏

☾ 07.20

AM

PM

Saturday 11
Sow leaf crops as the Moon chimes with Venus this morning.

♏

☾ 08.00

☾ ☍ ♀ 08.30

Sunday 12
Easter Sunday, the spring day of Resurrection.

♏ 15.00 ♐

☾ 08.50

☾ △ ☉ 12.50

Change 15.00

♎ Libra *Air*	♏ Scorpio *Water*	♐ Sagittarius *Fire*	♑ Capricorn *Earth*	♒ Aquarius *Air*	♓ Pisces *Water*

April 2020

Monday 13
Easter Monday

♐

℥ 04.00   PM only

☾ 09.40

Tuesday 14
Sow peas, beans and similar crops today.

♐ 21.00 ♑

◑

☾ 10.50

Wednesday 15
Sow onion sets, maincrop carrots and globe beetroot around noon.

♑

☾ ☌ ♄ 11.20

☾ 11.50

Thursday 16

♑

☾ 13.00

Friday 17

♑ 08.00 ♒

☾ ⚹ ☉ 15.30

☾ 14.10

Change 08.00

Saturday 18
A time to set up roses or perennial flower bushes, in the late afternoon.

♒

☾ □ ♀ 20.00

☾ 15.20

Sunday 19

♒ 20.00 ♓

☾ 16.20

Change 20.00

| ♀ Venus | ☉ Sun | △ Trine | ☌ Conjunction | ◓ Solar eclipse |
| ♄ Saturn | □ Square | ⚹ Sextile | ☍ Opposition | ◓ Lunar eclipse |

April 2020

Monday 20

♓

☾ ⚹ ♄ 11.20

☾ 17.30

⚇ 20.00

Tuesday 21

View the Lyrids meteor shower tonight.

♓

☾ ⚹ ♀ 12.20

☾ 18.40

Wednesday 22

Today is honoured as Earth Day.

♓ 09.00 ♈

☾ 19.40   *sow Courgettes!*

Change 09.00

Thursday 23

St George's Day

♈

● 03.00

☽ 06.00

Friday 24

The Islamic month of Ramadan begins, when Muslims fast during hours of daylight.

♈ 21.00 ♉

☽ 06.20

Saturday 25

♉

☽ △ ♄ 11.50

☽ 06.50

Sunday 26

♉

☽ ☌ ♀ 17.40

☽ 07.20

● New Moon	◑ 1st quarter	☽ Moonrise	☊ North node	⚇ Apogee
○ Full Moon	◐ 3rd quarter	☾ Moonset	☋ South node	℘ Perigee

April 2020

Monday 27

☿ 07.00 Ⅱ

☊ 19.00

AM only

☽ 08.00

Tuesday 28

Sow flowers as the Sun and Moon chime harmoniously together.

Ⅱ

☽ ⚹ ☉ 10.40

☽ 09.00

Wednesday 29

Ⅱ 15.00 ♋

☽ 10.00

Change 15.00

Thursday 30

Start some early cauliflowers (protected).

♋

☽ 11.10

♈	♉	Ⅱ	♋	♌	♍
Aries	Taurus	Gemini	Cancer	Leo	Virgo
Fire	*Earth*	*Air*	*Water*	*Fire*	*Earth*

May 2020

May Reminders

Friday 1

The pagan spring fire-festival of Beltane to mark the start of Summer. On May Day, a May Queen honours the fertility of the Earth. Party all night, if you can.

♋ 21.00 ♌

☽ ✶ ♀ 12.20

☽ 12.30

Saturday 2

♌

☽ 13.50

Sunday 3

♌ 23.00 ♍

☽ 15.10

May 2020

Monday 4

♍

☽△♄ 11.20

☽ 16.40

Tuesday 5

We are half-way between the Spring Equinox and the Summer Solstice.

♍ 23.00 ♎

☽△♀ 17.20

☽ 18.10

Wednesday 6

The mating of animals is best done around the Spring full moons.

♎

PM only

☽ 19.30

P 04.00

Thursday 7

A 'supermoon' is extra large, because its next to perigee.

♎ 23.00 ♏

○ 12.00

Friday 8

Early May bank holiday, moved this year to mark the 75th Anniversary of VE Day.

♏

☾✳♄ 11.30

☾ 05.50

Saturday 9

♏

☾ 06.30

Sunday 10

Mother's Day

♏ 01.00 ♐

No Planting

☋ 10.00

☾ 07.30

♀ Venus ⊙ Sun △ Trine ☌ Conjunction Solar eclipse

♄ Saturn □ Square ✳ Sextile ☍ Opposition Lunar eclipse

May 2020

Monday 11
Plant out late-flowering strawberries.

♐

☾ 08.30

Tuesday 12

♐ 06.00 ♑

☾ 09.40

Change 06.00

Wednesday 13

♑

☾ 10.50

Thursday 14

♑ 15.00 ♒

◐

☾ 12.00

☾ △ ♀ 10.20

Change 15.00

Friday 15
Prune lilac bushes after flowering.

♒

☾ 13.10

Saturday 16
The Sun meets the binary star Algol.

♒

☾ 14.10

Sunday 17

♒ 03.00 ♓

☾ 15.20

☾ ✶ ☉ 08.10

☾ ✶ ♄ 18.30

● New Moon	◐ 1st quarter	☽ Moonrise	☊ North node	*A* Apogee
○ Full Moon	◑ 3rd quarter	☾ Moonset	☋ South node	*P* Perigee

May 2020

Monday 18

♓

☾ 16.30
♌ 09.00

Tuesday 19

♓ 15.00 ♈

☾ ⚹ ♀ 09.20

☾ 17.30

Change 15.00

Wednesday 20

Sow runner beans and set up canes to support them.

♈

☾ 18.40

Thursday 21

♈

☾ 19.50

Friday 22

Draw up soil around early potatoes.

♈ 03.00 ♉

● 19.00

☾ △ ♄ 18.10

Saturday 23

The Islamic month of Ramadan ends.

♉

☽ 05.20

Sunday 24

Sow maincrop beetroot, swedes and turnips, and the last carrots on this root morning.

♉ 13.00 ♊

☊ 23.00

☽ 06.00

AM only

♈	♉	♊	♋	♌	♍
Aries	Taurus	Gemini	Cancer	Leo	Virgo
Fire	*Earth*	*Air*	*Water*	*Fire*	*Earth*

May 2020

Monday 25
Spring bank holiday

♊

☽ 06.50

Tuesday 26
Sow hardy annual flowers and
plant out when all possible risk
of frost has passed.

♊ 21.00 ♋

☽ 07.50

Wednesday 27
Sow spinach and cabbage this
morning.

♋

☽ ⚹ ☉ 20.00

☽ 09.00

Thursday 28
Venus vanishes from view as the
Evening Star.

♋

☽ ⚹ ♀ 14.30

☽ 10.20

Friday 29

♋ 02.00 ♌

☽ 11.40

Saturday 30
Continue to sow dwarf and
runner beans.

♌

◑

☽ 13.00

Sunday 31
The Sun meets the rose-pink
star Aldebaran, the 'Bulls-Eye',
bringing good fortune.

♌ 06.00 ♍

☽ △ ♄ 18.20

☽ 14.20

Change 06.00

♎	♏	♐	♑	♒	♓
Libra	Scorpio	Sagittarius	Capricorn	Aquarius	Pisces
Air	*Water*	*Fire*	*Earth*	*Air*	*Water*

June 2020

Monday 1

♍
☽ 15.40
☽△☉ 10.30
☽△♀ 16.20

Tuesday 2

♍ 07.00 ♎
☽ 17.10
Change 07.00

Wednesday 3

Sow hardy wild flowers and wallflowers in late afternoon. Hoe for weeds.

♎
☽ 18.30
p 05.00
PM only

Thursday 4

♎ 09.00 ♏
☽ 19.50
Change 09.00

Friday 5

Partial lunar eclipse, stay away from the garden.

♏
○ (lunar eclipse) 20.00
☾☍♀ 15.00
No Planting

Saturday 6

Pick out shoots on aromatics such as rosemary to encourage growth.

♏ 11.00 ♐
☾ 05.10
☋ 19.00
AM only

Sunday 7

♐
☾ 06.10

♀ Venus
♄ Saturn
☉ Sun
□ Square
△ Trine
⚹ Sextile
☌ Conjunction
☍ Opposition
Solar eclipse
Lunar eclipse

June 2020

Monday 8

♐ 15.00 ♑

☾ 07.20

Change 15.00

Tuesday 9

Venus appears as the Morning Star.

♑

☾ 08.30

Wednesday 10

♑ 23.00 ♒

☾ △ ☉ 15.30

☾ 09.40

Thursday 11

♒

☾ 10.50

Friday 12

♒

☾ 12.00

Saturday 13

♒ 10.00 ♓

◑

☾ 13.10

Change 10.00

Sunday 14

Thin out lettuces and use the seedlings in salads.

♓

☾ ⚹ ♀ 13.20

☾ 14.10

● New Moon   ◑ 1st quarter   ☽ Moonrise   ☊ North node   𝒜 Apogee
○ Full Moon   ◐ 3rd quarter   ☾ Moonset   ☋ South node   𝒫 Perigee

June 2020

Monday 15

♓ 23.00 ♈

☾ 15.20

♫ 02.00

Tuesday 16

♈

☾ 16.30

Wednesday 17

♈

☾ 17.30

Thursday 18

♈ 11.00 ♉

☾ 18.40

Change 11.00

Friday 19

See the last of the dying old moon after sunset.

♉

☾ ♂ ♀ 09.40

☾ 19.50

Saturday 20

Summer Solstice (exact at 10.45 pm): celebrate the longest day with friends.

♉ 20.00 ♊

☾ 20.50

Change 20.00

Sunday 21

Solar eclipse, no gardening today.

♊

☉ ◗ 08.00

● 07.00

☋ 05.00

No Planting

♈	♉	♊	♋	♌	♍
Aries	Taurus	Gemini	Cancer	Leo	Virgo
Fire	*Earth*	*Air*	*Water*	*Fire*	*Earth*

June 2020

Monday 22
Notice how low the midsummer Full Moon is in the night sky.

♊

☽ 05.40

Tuesday 23
Midsummer's Eve, St John's Eve

♊ 03.00 ♋

☽ 06.50

Wednesday 24
St John's Day. Look for the St John's Wort plant coming into blossom.

♋

☽ 08.10

Thursday 25

♋ 08.00 ♌

☽ 09.30

Change 08.00

Friday 26
Tend to fruit trees in the morning, around 11 am.

♌

☽ 10.50

Saturday 27

♌ 11.00 ♍

☽ 12.10

Change 11.00

Sunday 28
Take softwood cuttings of shrubs to make new plants.

♍

◑

☽ △ ♀ 06.30

☽ 13.30

♎	♏	♐	♑	♒	♓
Libra	Scorpio	Sagittarius	Capricorn	Aquarius	Pisces
Air	Water	Fire	Earth	Air	Water

June 2020

Monday 29

♍ 14.00 ♎

☽ 14.50

AM

PM

Tuesday 30

Plant Brussels sprouts, winter cabbage, savoys and purple sprouting broccoli.

♎

☽ 16.10

♇ 03.00

☽ △ ☉ 15.20

PM only

Gardening Notes

♀ Venus	☉ Sun	△ Trine	♂ Conjunction	● Solar eclipse
♄ Saturn	□ Square	✳ Sextile	☍ Opposition	☾ Lunar eclipse

July 2020

July Reminders

Wednesday 1	♎ 16.00 ♏		🌼
	☽ 17.30		Change 16.00
			🍃

Thursday 2	♏		
		☽ ☌ ♀ 13.00	🍃
	☽ 18.50		

Friday 3	♏ 20.00 ♐		🍃
	☽ 20.00		Change 20.00
			🍊

Saturday 4
Aphelion near 1 pm, when the Earth is at its furthest point from the Sun.

♐
☊ 04.00   PM only 🍊
☽ 21.00

Sunday 5
Partial lunar eclipse, no gardening today.

♐
○ ☌ 06.00   No Planting
X

| ● New Moon | ◑ 1st quarter | ☽ Moonrise | ☊ North node | 𝒜 Apogee |
| ○ Full Moon | ◑ 3rd quarter | ☾ Moonset | ☋ South node | 𝒫 Perigee |

July 2020

Monday 6

♐ 01.00 ♑

☽ ☌ ♄ 10.40

☽ 06.10

Tuesday 7

Sow root vegetables such as turnips for winter use.

♑

☽ 07.20

Wednesday 8

♑ 08.00 ♒

☽ 08.30

Change 08.00

Thursday 9

Plant flowers at the moonrise hour of 10 am, or later at noon for the Venus-aspect.

♒

☽ □ ♀ 12.10

☽ 09.40

Friday 10

♒ 18.00 ♓

☽ △ ☉ 07.10

☽ 10.50

Change 18.00

Saturday 11

♓

☽ 12.00

Sunday 12

♓

☽ 13.00

♈ 20.00

♈	♉	♊	♋	♌	♍
Aries	Taurus	Gemini	Cancer	Leo	Virgo
Fire	Earth	Air	Water	Fire	Earth

July 2020

Monday 13
Pinch out side-shoots on tomatoes in the afternoon.

♓ 07.00 ♈
◑
☾ 14.10

Change 07.00

Tuesday 14

♈
☾ 15.20

Wednesday 15

♈ 19.00 ♉
☾ ✳ ☉ 17.50
☾ 16.30

Change 19.00

Thursday 16
Continue to sow root veg for winter use, and earth-up maincrop potatoes.

♉
☾ 17.30

Friday 17

♉
☾ ☌ ♀ 07.40
☾ 18.40

Saturday 18

♉ 05.00 ♊
☊ 14.00
☾ 19.30

No Planting

✗

Sunday 19
Spend a quiet Sunday afternoon tending flower beds.

♊
☾ 20.20

♎	♏	♐	♑	♒	♓
Libra	Scorpio	Sagittarius	Capricorn	Aquarius	Pisces
Air	*Water*	*Fire*	*Earth*	*Air*	*Water*

July 2020

Monday 20
Saturn is at its brightest around this time.

♊ 11.00 ♋
● 19.00

Change 11.00

Tuesday 21

♋

☽ 05.50

Wednesday 22

♋ 15.00 ♌

☽ 07.10

Change 15.00

Thursday 23
Use the Moonrise hour of 8–9 am to work with fruit-seed crops.

♌

☽ 08.30

Friday 24

♌ 17.00 ♍

☽ 09.50

Change 17.00

Saturday 25

♍

☽ ✶ ☉ 07.30

PM only

☽ 11.10
℗ 06.00

Sunday 26

♍ 19.00 ♎

☽ △ ♀ 11.40

☽ 12.40

Change 19.00

♀ Venus	☉ Sun	△ Trine	♂ Conjunction	● Solar eclipse
♄ Saturn	□ Square	✶ Sextile	☍ Opposition	Lunar eclipse

July 2020

Monday 27

♎︎
◑
☽ 14.00

Tuesday 28

♎︎ 22.00 ♏︎
☽ 15.20

Wednesday 29

♏︎
☽ ✶ ♄ 05.00
☽ 16.40

Thursday 30

Sow lettuce and greens for winter use: leeks, late Brussels sprouts, winter cabbage, spring broccoli.

♏︎
☽ 17.50

Friday 31

Take a day off, the Moon crossing over its node is a bad time for gardening.

♏︎ 03.00 ♐︎
☋ 11.00
☽ 18.50

No Planting

X

Gardening Notes

● New Moon ◐ 1st quarter ☽ Moonrise ☊ North node 𝒜 Apogee
○ Full Moon ◑ 3rd quarter ☾ Moonset ☋ South node 𝒫 Perigee

August 2020

August Reminders

Saturday 1

Today is Lammas, the old English festival to mark the wheat harvest. Mark the occasion with a barbecue.

♐

☽ 19.40

Sunday 2

♐ 08.00 ♑

☽♂♄ 15.00

☽ 20.10

Change 08.00

♈	♉	♊	♋	♌	♍
Aries	Taurus	Gemini	Cancer	Leo	Virgo
Fire	*Earth*	*Air*	*Water*	*Fire*	*Earth*

August 2020

Monday 3

♑
○ 17.00

Tuesday 4
Venus reaches its highest point in the early morning sky.

♑ 16.00 ♒
☾ 06.10

Change 16.00

Wednesday 5

♒
☾ 07.20

Thursday 6
Sow wallflowers and sweet Williams for next year, and set out seedlings and perennials.

♒
☾ 08.30

Friday 7
We are mid-way between the Summer Solstice and the Autumn Equinox.

♒ 02.00 ♓
☾ ⚹ ♄ 08.50
☾ 09.40

Saturday 8
Transplant flower seedlings this morning, plant daffodils and take cuttings from rambling roses.

♓
☾ 10.50

Sunday 9

♓ 15.00 ♈
☾ 12.00
⚹ 15.00

Change 15.00

♎	♏	♐	♑	♒	♓
Libra	Scorpio	Sagittarius	Capricorn	Aquarius	Pisces
Air	*Water*	*Fire*	*Earth*	*Air*	*Water*

August 2020

Monday 10
Re-pot tomatoes sown in June. Prepare the ground for planting new fruit stocks, and complete the planting of strawberry runners.

♈

☽ ✳ ♀ 07.20

☽ 13.00

Tuesday 11
Prune the fruited shoots of peach and plum trees.

♈

◑

☽ 14.10

Wednesday 12
The Perseids meteor shower, coming from the Perseus constellation, is visible after midnight.

♈ 03.00 ♉

☽ △ ♄ 08.50

☽ 15.20

Thursday 13

♉

☽ 16.20

Friday 14

♉ 14.00 ♊

☽ ✳ ☉ 09.30

☊ 20.00

AM only

☽ 17.20

Saturday 15

♊

☽ ♂ ♀ 14.30

☽ 18.10

Sunday 16

♊ 20.00 ♋

Change 20.00

☽ 19.00

| ♀ Venus | ☉ Sun | △ Trine | ♂ Conjunction | ◖ Solar eclipse |
| ♄ Saturn | ☐ Square | ✳ Sextile | ☍ Opposition | ◗ Lunar eclipse |

August 2020

Monday 17

♋

Sow lettuce and greens for winter, leeks, late Brussels sprouts, winter cabbage and spring broccoli.

☾ 19.30

Tuesday 18

♋ 24.00 ♌

☾ 20.00

Wednesday 19

♌

● 04.00

☽ 06.10

Thursday 20

♌

Sow herbs or seed crops in the morning. Islamic New Year.

☽ ⚹ ♀ 05.10

☽ 07.30

Friday 21

♌ 01.00 ♍

No Planting

☽ 09.00

𝑃 12.00

X

Saturday 22

♍

The Sun meets Regulus, for millennia the brightest star in the constellation Leo.

☽ 10.20

Sunday 23

♍ 02.00 ♎

☽ ⚹ ☉ 12.30

☽ 11.40

● New Moon   ◑ 1st quarter   ☽ Moonrise   ♌ North node   𝒜 Apogee

○ Full Moon   ◑ 3rd quarter   ☾ Moonset   ☋ South node   𝑃 Perigee

August 2020

Monday 24

♎︎

☽ 13.10

☽ △ ♀ 14.50

Tuesday 25

Sow winter spinach, spring cabbage and hardy lettuce today.

♎︎ 04.00 ♏︎

◑

☽ 14.30

☽ ✶ ♄ 07.30

Wednesday 26

♏︎

☽ 15.40

Thursday 27

♏︎ 08.00 ♐︎

♉︎ 13.00

☽ 16.40

No Planting

X

Friday 28

Harvest crops on the days coming up to this Harvest Moon, whether for sale or use.

♐︎

☽ 17.30

Saturday 29

♐︎ 15.00 ♑︎

☽ 18.10

☽ ☍ ♀ 09.50

☽ ♂ ♄ 18.20

Change 15.00

Sunday 30

♑︎

☽ 18.50

♈︎	♉︎	♊︎	♋︎	♌︎	♍︎
Aries	Taurus	Gemini	Cancer	Leo	Virgo
Fire	*Earth*	*Air*	*Water*	*Fire*	*Earth*

August 2020

Monday 31
Summer bank holiday

♑ 23.00 ♒

☽ 19.10

Gardening Notes ———————————————

September 2020

Tuesday 1
Transplant flower seedlings, and take cuttings from rambler roses, in late afternoon.

♒

☽ 19.30

Wednesday 2
At dusk, see the golden orb of the Harvest Moon. How large and low it appears amongst the autumn mists.

♒

○ 06.00

Thursday 3
Tend to trees today, with the fine Saturn and Venus aspects.

♒ 10.00 ♓

☾ 07.30

☾ ✶ ♄ 13.10

☾ △ ♀ 15.30

Change 10.00

Friday 4

♓

☾ 08.40

Saturday 5
Prune trees in the waning Moon.

♓ 22.00 ♈

☾ 09.40

Sunday 6
Farmers, harvest the golden grain.

♈

☾ 10.50

♃ 07.00

♀ Venus   ☉ Sun   △ Trine   ♂ Conjunction   ☾ Solar eclipse

♄ Saturn   ☐ Square   ✶ Sextile   ☍ Opposition   ☽ Lunar eclipse

September 2020

Monday 7

Pick early apples and pears while slightly under-ripe, and transplant or work with any fruit crops.

♈

☾ △ ⊙ 17.10

☾ 12.00

Tuesday 8

♈ 11.00 ♉

☾ △ ♄ 13.50

☾ 13.00

Change 11.00

Wednesday 9

Sow winter radishes and harvest onions when the tops have died down, around 2 pm.

♉

☾ 14.10

Thursday 10

Lift and store potatoes, beets and carrots.

♉ 22.00 ♊

◑

☾ 15.10

Friday 11

♊

☊ 00.00

PM only

☾ 16.00

Saturday 12

Scatter wood ash on to rose beds and hoe it, around 5 pm. Start planting bulbs today as well.

♊

☾ 16.50

Sunday 13

♊ 06.00 ♋

☾ 17.30

Change 06.00

● New Moon	◑ 1st quarter	☽ Moonrise	☊ North node	𝒜 Apogee
○ Full Moon	◐ 3rd quarter	☾ Moonset	☋ South node	𝑃 Perigee

September 2020

Monday 14
Sow parsley and chervil, and varieties of lettuce for over wintering in cloches.

♋

☾ ♂ ♀ 07.50

☾ 18.00

Tuesday 15

♋ 10.00 ♌

☾ 18.30

Change 10.00

Wednesday 16
Harvest crops for storage over winter.

♌

☾ 18.50

Thursday 17

♌ 11.00 ♍

● 12.00

☾ △ ♄ 12.40

Change 11.00

Friday 18
Jewish New Year

♍

☽ ⚹ ♀ 17.40

☽ 07.50

𝘱 15.00

No Planting

X

Saturday 19

♍ 10.00 ♎

☽ 09.20

Change 10.00

Sunday 20
Use the Moonrise hour to sow annuals in the greenhouse for a spring display.

♎

☽ 10.50

♈	♉	♊	♋	♌	♍
Aries	Taurus	Gemini	Cancer	Leo	Virgo
Fire	Earth	Air	Water	Fire	Earth

September 2020

Monday 21

♎︎ 11.00 ♏︎

☽ ✳ ♄ 12.50
☽ 12.10
☽ ✳ ☉ 19.10

Change 11.00

Tuesday 22

Autumn Equinox. Honour this time by telling the seasonal story of Demeter and Persephone.

♏︎

☽ 13.30

Wednesday 23

♏︎ 14.00 ♐︎

☋ 14.00

☽ 14.40

No Planting

X

Thursday 24

♐︎

◑

☽ 15.30

Friday 25

♐︎ 20.00 ♑︎

☽ 16.20

Change 20.00

Saturday 26

♑︎

☽ △ ☉ 14.30

☽ 16.50

Sunday 27

Celebrate the Harvest festival.

♑︎

☽ 17.20

♎︎	♏︎	♐︎	♑︎	♒︎	♓︎
Libra	Scorpio	Sagittarius	Capricorn	Aquarius	Pisces
Air	Water	Fire	Earth	Air	Water

September 2020

Monday 28

♑ 05.00 ♒

☽ ☍ ♀ 06.00

Change 05.00

☽ 17.40

Tuesday 29

Michaelmas Day

♒

☽ 18.00

Wednesday 30

Tend to and graft trees, use the
Saturn-aspect in late afternoon.

♒ 16.00 ♓

☽ ✶ ♄ 18.30

Change 16.00

☽ 18.10

Gardening Notes

| ♀ Venus | ☉ Sun | △ Trine | ♂ Conjunction | Solar eclipse |
| ♄ Saturn | □ Square | ✶ Sextile | ☍ Opposition | Lunar eclipse |

October 2020

October Reminders

Thursday 1

Hunter's Moon, when hunters in years gone by would appreciate the Full Moon at dusk.

♓

○ 22.00

☽ 18.30

Friday 2

Plant winter lettuce in the morning. Force-grow rhubarb in a warm greenhouse.

♓

☾ 07.30

Saturday 3

♓ 04.00 ♈

☾△♀ 18.10

☾ 08.40

𝒜 18.00

Sunday 4

Pick and store apples and pears as they mature. Cut out the fruited blackberry and loganberry canes and train in new shoots.

♈

☾ 09.50

● New Moon	◑ 1st quarter	☽ Moonrise	♌ North node	𝒜 Apogee
○ Full Moon	◑ 3rd quarter	☾ Moonset	☋ South node	𝒫 Perigee

October 2020

Monday 5

♈ 17.00 ♉

☾ △ ♄ 19.40

☾ 10.50

Change 17.00

Tuesday 6

♉

☾ 12.00

Wednesday 7

Lift and store beetroot, dig up maincrop potatoes.

♉

☾ △ ☉ 10.20

☾ 13.00

Thursday 8

♉ 05.00 ♊

☋ 01.00

PM only

☾ 14.00

Friday 9

Prepare new rose beds for planting; plant lily-of-the-valley. Plant out herbaceous perennials.

♊

☾ ⚹ ♀ 07.20

☾ 14.40

Saturday 10

♊ 15.00 ♋

◐

☾ 15.20

Change 15.00

Sunday 11

Start planting winter lettuce around 4 pm, and force-grow rhubarb in a warm greenhouse.

♋

☾ 16.00

♈	♉	♊	♋	♌	♍
Aries	Taurus	Gemini	Cancer	Leo	Virgo
Fire	*Earth*	*Air*	*Water*	*Fire*	*Earth*

October 2020

Monday 12

♋ 20.00 ♌

☾ ✶ ☉ 12.10

☾ 16.30

Change 20.00

Tuesday 13

Continue to pick tomatoes, and let them ripen in trays. Work on any fruit trees.

♌

☾ 16.50

Wednesday 14

Can you spot the red planet Mars shining at its brightest in the dark night sky?

♌ 22.00 ♍

☾ 17.10

Thursday 15

At the dark of the Moon, pick crops to store over winter: potatoes, carrots and beetroot.

♍

☾ 17.30

Friday 16

The Sun passes by Spica today, the benevolent star of the grain harvest.

♍ 21.00 ♎

● 21.00

☾ 18.00

Saturday 17

♎

PM only

☽ 08.10

♇ 01.00

Sunday 18

♎ 20.00 ♏

☽ ✶ ♀ 11.00

Change 20.00

☽ 09.40

♎	♏	♐	♑	♒	♓
Libra	Scorpio	Sagittarius	Capricorn	Aquarius	Pisces
Air	*Water*	*Fire*	*Earth*	*Air*	*Water*

October 2020

Monday 19

♏

☽ 11.10

Tuesday 20

♏ 22.00 ♐

☋ 17.00

No Planting

X

☽ 12.20

Wednesday 21

Continue to pick and store apples and pears as they mature. Train new blackberry shoots.

♐

☽ 13.30

Thursday 22

♐

☽ 14.10

Friday 23

♐ 03.00 ♑

◐

☽☌♄ 05.30

☽ 14.50

Saturday 24

♑

☽ 15.20

Sunday 25

End of British Summer Time: clocks go back one hour.

♑ 10.00 ♒

Change 10.00

☽ 14.40

♀ Venus	⊙ Sun	△ Trine	☌ Conjunction	Solar eclipse
♄ Saturn	□ Square	⚹ Sextile	☍ Opposition	Lunar eclipse

October 2020

Monday 26

♒

☽ 15.00

Tuesday 27

Prepare new rose-beds for planting.

♒ 21.00 ♓

☽ 15.20

Wednesday 28

♓

☽ ☍ ♀ 09.30

☽ 15.40

Thursday 29

Plant herbaceous perennials and deciduous trees, but avoid frosty conditions.

♓

☽ 15.50

Friday 30

♓ 9.00 ♈

☽ 16.10

𝒜 19.00

Change 09.00

Saturday 31

A Blue Moon as it's the second full moon this month. Halloween, traditionally a time of otherwordly inteference in human affairs.

♈

○ 15.00

● New Moon   ◑ 1st quarter   ☽ Moonrise   ☊ North node   𝒜 Apogee
○ Full Moon   ◑ 3rd quarter   ☾ Moonset   ☋ South node   𝒫 Perigee

November 2020

November Reminders ─────────

Sunday 1
All Saints' Day

♈ 22.00 ♉

☾ 07.40

♈	♉	♊	♋	♌	♍
Aries	Taurus	Gemini	Cancer	Leo	Virgo
Fire	*Earth*	*Air*	*Water*	*Fire*	*Earth*

November 2020

Monday 2
♉
☾ 08.50

Tuesday 3
Compost the fallen leaves as you clear them.
♉
☾ 09.50

Wednesday 4
♉ 10.00 ♊
☊ 03.00
☾ 10.50
PM only

Thursday 5
♊
☾ □ ♀ 18.20
☾ 11.40

Friday 6
The pagan quarter-day of Samhain, a gathering of the clans before winter begins: mid-way between Autumn Equinox and Winter Solstice.
♊ 20.00 ♋
☾ 12.20
Change 20.00

Saturday 7
♋
☾ 13.00

Sunday 8
♋
◐
☾ ⚹ ♀ 08.40
☾ 13.30

♎	♏	♐	♑	♒	♓
Libra	Scorpio	Sagittarius	Capricorn	Aquarius	Pisces
Air	*Water*	*Fire*	*Earth*	*Air*	*Water*

November 2020

Monday 9
Plant gooseberry bushes and raspberry canes; sow peas and prune trees.

♋ 03.00 ♌

☾ 13.50

Tuesday 10

♌

☾ 14.10

Wednesday 11

♌ 07.00 ♍

☾△♄ 11.00

☾ 14.30

Change 07.00

Thursday 12

♍

☾ 15.00

Friday 13

♍ 07.00 ♎

☾ 15.20

Change 07.00

Saturday 14
The Indian festival of Diwali begins, light some candles to celebrate the conquest of good over evil.

♎

☾ 15.50

♇ 12.00

No Planting

X

Sunday 15
Pick herbs to dry. Take cuttings of bay and rue and and place in pots of sand. Re-pot mint in the greenhouse.

♎ 06.00 ♏

● 05.00

☽✶♄ 11.10

☽ 07.30

Change 06.00

| ♀ Venus | ☉ Sun | △ Trine | ♂ Conjunction | ☌ Solar eclipse |
| ♄ Saturn | ☐ Square | ✶ Sextile | ☍ Opposition | ☌ Lunar eclipse |

November 2020

Monday 16

♏

☽ 09.00

Tuesday 17

♏ 07.00 ♐

☋ 00.00

☽ 10.10

☽ ✶ ♀ 07.50

PM only

Wednesday 18

♐

☽ 11.10

Thursday 19

♐ 10.00 ♑

☽ ☌ ♄ 15.50

Change 10.00

☽ 11.50

☽ ✶ ☉ 16.30

Friday 20

♑

☽ 12.20

Saturday 21

The Moon moves from Earth (root-crop) to Air (flowers) this afternoon.

♑ 17.00 ♒

Change 17.00

☽ 12.50

Sunday 22

Cut back and tidy any flowering plants in the afternoon, in the greenhouse. Start forcing bulbs and sow seed of most alpines.

♒

◐

☽ △ ♀ 05.40

☽ 13.10

● New Moon ◐ 1st quarter ☽ Moonrise ☊ North node 𝒜 Apogee

○ Full Moon ◑ 3rd quarter ☾ Moonset ☋ South node 𝒫 Perigee

November 2020

Monday 23

♒︎

☽ 13.30

Tuesday 24

Clear fallen leaves and pile up for leaf mould.

♒︎ 03.00 ♓︎

☽ ✶ ♄ 10.40

☽ 13.40

Wednesday 25

Use the Moonrise hour to lift chicory and asparagus.

♓︎

☽ 14.00

Thursday 26

♓︎ 16.00 ♈︎

☽ 14.20

Change 16.00

Friday 27

Sow broad beans if the soil is dry and over-winter under cloches.

♈︎

☽ ☍ ♀ 19.20

☽ 14.40

𝒜 00.00

Saturday 28

Plant fruit trees and bushes, soak dry tree roots before planting, and prune fruit trees after planting. Stake trees.

♈︎

☽ 15.00

Sunday 29

Advent Sunday; Christmas decorations can go up now.

♈︎ 05.00 ♉︎

☽ △ ♄ 12.50

☽ 15.30

Change 05.00

♈︎	♉︎	♊︎	♋︎	♌︎	♍︎
Aries	Taurus	Gemini	Cancer	Leo	Virgo
Fire	*Earth*	*Air*	*Water*	*Fire*	*Earth*

November 2020

Monday 30

Partial lunar eclipse, stay out of the garden. St Andrew's Day, a national holiday in Scotland.

♉

○ ☋ 09.00

No Planting

Gardening Notes

♎︎	♏︎	♐︎	♑︎	♒︎	♓︎
Libra	Scorpio	Sagittarius	Capricorn	Aquarius	Pisces
Air	*Water*	*Fire*	*Earth*	*Air*	*Water*

December 2020

| **Tuesday 1** | ♂ 16.00 ♊ | | PM only |
| | ☾ 08.50 | ☊ 08.00 | ❀ |

| **Wednesday 2** | ♊ | | |
| | ☾ 09.40 | | ❀ |

| **Thursday 3**
Finish planting roses in the morning. | ♊ | ☾ △ ♀ 07.40 | |
| | ☾ 10.20 | | ❀ |

| **Friday 4**
Trim back lawn edges to make the garden tidy. | ♊ 02.00 ♋ | | |
| | ☾ 11.00 | | 🍃 |

| **Saturday 5** | ♋ | ☾ △ ☉ 14.40 | |
| | ☾ 11.30 | | 🍃 |

| **Sunday 6**
St Nicholas's Day | ♋ 09.00 ♌ | ☽ ✶ ☉ 13.40 | Change 09.00 |
| | ☾ 12.00 | | 🍋 |

| ♀ Venus | ☉ Sun | △ Trine | ♂ Conjunction | ☌ Solar eclipse |
| ♄ Saturn | ☐ Square | ✶ Sextile | ☍ Opposition | ☌ Lunar eclipse |

December 2020

Monday 7
Work on vines or other fruits in the greenhouse. Sow melons around noon for an early crop

♌

☾ 12.20

Tuesday 8
♌ 14.00 ♍

◑

☾ ✳ ♀ 08.20

☾ 12.40

AM

PM

Wednesday 9
Check over any stored corns or tubers for signs of mould. Sow carrots in frames.

♍

☾ 13.00

Thursday 10
♍ 16.00 ♎

☾ ✳ ☉ 07.20

☾ 13.20

Change 16.00

Friday 11
♎

☾ 13.40

Saturday 12
Prick out any prerennials you have raised in the greenhouse and sow winter bedding plants.

♎ 17.00 ♏

☾ 14.10

ρ 21.00

AM only

Sunday 13
♏

☾ 14.50

● New Moon   ◐ 1st quarter   ☽ Moonrise   ♌ North node   𝒜 Apogee
○ Full Moon   ◑ 3rd quarter   ☾ Moonset   ☋ South node   ρ Perigee

December 2020

Monday 14
Total solar eclipse, stay out of the garden. The Geminids meteor shower may reach its maximum during this dark night, weather permitting.

♏ 18.00 ♐
●● 16.00
☾ 15.40

♋ 11.00

No Planting

✗

Tuesday 15
♐

☽ 08.50

Wednesday 16
♐ 20.00 ♑

☽ 09.40

Change 20.00

Thursday 17
Dig in compost, and cover heavy land with well-rotted compost.

♑

☽ 10.20

☽ ☌ ♄ 06.30
☽ ✶ ♀ 10.20

Friday 18
Finish digging new beds and borders for winter weathering.

♑

☽ 10.50

☊ 14.00

Saturday 19
Finish planting roses and prune back established beds.

♑ 02.00 ♒

☽ 11.10

☽ ✶ ☉ 08.40

Sunday 20
♒

☽ 11.30

♈	♉	♊	♋	♌	♍
Aries	Taurus	Gemini	Cancer	Leo	Virgo
Fire	Earth	Air	Water	Fire	Earth

December 2020

Monday 21
Winter Solstice, the shortest day and longest night.

♒ 11.00 ♓
◑
☽ 11.50

Change 11.00

Tuesday 22

♓
☽ △ ♀ 16.00
☽ 12.10

Wednesday 23
Plant new hedges, shrubs and trees.

♓ 23.00 ♈
☽ 12.20

Thursday 24

♈
☽ △ ☉ 17.50
☽ 12.40
A 17.00

Friday 25
Christmas Day and the twelve Holy Nights begin.

♈
☽ 13.00

Saturday 26
Boxing Day

♈ 12.00 ♉
☽ 13.30

AM

PM

Sunday 27

♉
☽ 14.00

♎	♏	♐	♑	♒	♓
Libra	Scorpio	Sagittarius	Capricorn	Aquarius	Pisces
Air	*Water*	*Fire*	*Earth*	*Air*	*Water*

December 2020

Monday 28
Substitute Bank Holiday for Boxing Day in England & Wales.

♉ 23.00 ♊

☽☍♀ 06.50

☽ 14.40 ☊ 15.00

No Planting

X

Tuesday 29

♊

☽ 15.30

Wednesday 30
Midwinter Full Moon

♊

○ 03.00

☾ 08.20

Thursday 31
New Year's Eve (Hogmanay in Scotland)

♊ 8.00 ♋

Change 08.00

☾ 09.00

Gardening Notes

♀ Venus ⊙ Sun △ Trine ☌ Conjunction Solar eclipse

♄ Saturn □ Square ⚹ Sextile ☍ Opposition Lunar eclipse

The Seasons of

2020

Young Spring was there, his head encircled with a flowery garland, and Summer, lightly clad, crowned with a wreath of corn ears; Autumn too, stained purple with treading out the vintage, and icy Winter, with white and shaggy locks.

Ovid

The year 2020 begins with Perihelion on 5 January – this is the time when the Earth is at its nearest point to the Sun. Reflect upon the paradox of the planet being at its closest to the Sun in deep midwinter – at least, in the Northern hemisphere. A few days later comes the first lunar eclipse of the year. Chinese New Year is early this year on 25 January, after the New Moon the day before. The Chinese have the most sensible time to start the year, on the New Moon nearest to the quarter-day that we call Imbolc. One is then supposed to pay off debts, clean out the clutter from home and, if you can, join in the festival of the Red Dragon in your nearest Chinatown!

For pagans, February opens with the Imbolc fire-festival, also the feast of the Celtic goddess Brid, on 4 February. This signifies the promise or the first glimpse of spring, when the first snowdrops appear, when ewes begin to lactate and will soon give birth to the spring lambs. This was also the time when farmers would 'beat the bounds' of their land, in which they performed a ceremonial perambulation of their boundary. A couple of days earlier are the parallel festivals of Groundhog Day in the US and Candlemas in the Christian calendar, which both signify winter's end. Many of the pagan festivals were absorbed into the Christian traditions, leading to a melding of pagan and Christian significance. Many rustic proverbs cluster around this day, for example, from Germany, 'The badger peeps out of his hole on Candlemas Day/And if he finds snow, walks abroad/But if he sees the sun shining/ Draws back into his hole'. Later in February comes *Mardi Gras*, which is Shrove Tuesday in the Christian calendar, which comes just after the New Moon. A New Moon is a proper time for beginnings.

Still early in the year we see Venus as the brilliant Evening Star. It rises highest in the sky in March, and then grows most brilliant in April. After that its brightness will gradually fade, until it dies down into the sunset in late May. If you live away from city lights, try to have a party in springtime where your guests can admire the Evening Star. It comes nearest to Earth when invisible to our eyes in early June, then reappears later that month as the Morning Star. The lovely old English word for the Morning Star was used by Tolkein in his epic *Lord of the Rings*, 'Hail Eärendil, brightest of stars'. Farmers up before dawn may wish to meditate upon the Roman name Lucifer, which meant 'light-bringer' – at Venus's pre-dawn appearance the stars were put to flight.

Hindu New Year comes a day after the New Moon of March, while the Persian New Year is sensibly fixed on the spring equinox on 20 March. The festival of St Patrick's Day is a few days earlier, but our Calendar is more focused on the lunar-defined events which make up the ancient sacred calendars of humanity. In 2020, March and April both enjoy 'supermoons' – when the Moon is on or near to its perigee and therefore appears extra large.

Christian Holy Week centres around the Full Moon of 8 April, after the spring equinox. On the New Moon two weeks later the Islamic month of Ramadan begins, a time of fast for Muslims who are not allowed to eat or drink while the Sun is above the horizon. That holy month starts when the first sliver of the New Moon is seen, which our calendar usually puts on the second day after the astronomical New Moon.

The pagan fire-festival of Beltane falls on 6 May, which is followed by the May bank holiday on 8 May. This 'quarter-day' midway between the solstices and equinoxes is a time to mull over the eightfold structure of the year: this festival is the start of summer, not the middle of spring. This is a life-affirming fire-festival, to honour the fertility of spring. Farm animals lactate, and sheep and cattle are put out to summer pastures. Be up to greet the dawn and early-morning mists – after an all-night party, if you can! See if your community can manage a May Queen and a maypole, to invoke a festive spirit. Beltane this year synchronises with the Full Moon – which is also the springtime Buddhist festival of Wesak, to honour the Buddha's birthday.

The midsummer solstice chimes on 20 June, when Earth and Sun then align with the galaxy on that longest day and the Sun crosses over the Galactic Equator. If you have a St John's Wort plant, check if it has opened up, as it should, on St John's Day, 24 June. This flower is traditionally used to treat depression. Note how this day is three days after the summer solstice, just as Christmas comes three days after the winter solstice. This is when the Sun starts to move again as seen on the horizon – it 'stands still' on the solstice, that's what the word means.

July begins with Aphelion, when the Earth is furthest away from the Sun in its yearly course. Here is another paradox: we feel the warmest summer heat when the planet is furthest from the Sun. Perhaps mark the Lammas Full Moon of early August with a barbecue with your friends and experience the Full Moon rising as the Sun sets. Lammas is summertime holiday period, a 'gathering of the tribes' and the word alludes to the loaf made from the first new wheat, so this summer's-end festival also marks the start of the harvest, and the end of the crop-circle season! On the 13 August watch the Perseids meteor shower after midnight. The New Moon of 19 August brings the start of Islamic New Year.

In early September comes the Harvest Moon, big and yellow near to the horizon. Two weeks later it's the Jewish New Year at the New Moon. The autumn equinox tips us into the dark half of the year, and that is a time to recall the story of how Demeter, the earth or corn-goddess, then loses her lovely daughter Persephone, who will reappear six months later.

The start of October brings the Hunter's Moon rising, in the 'season of mists and mellow fruitfulness'. The Sun is passing through the sidereal sign of the Balance over this period, until 17 October – that's the same zodiac system used in this Calendar for the Moon. Two days later on the first Sunday of October is the Harvest festival.

Samhain, (pronounced 'sawain') on 7 November marks the Celtic New Year, it was the last chance for the clans to meet before winter. Our modern equivalents are Hallowe'en – mischief night! – and Bonfire Night. Nature dies back for another year and brings an other-worldly flavour to this time of supernatural interference in human affairs: ghosts, ghouls and divination.

Sacred Moons of 2020

In our multi-cultural society it makes sense to honour the sacred moons of different cultures. The calendars of several of the great religions are founded on the lunar cycle and lunar-based sacred calendars still exist around the world. Many cultures begin their year on a New Moon, which is the proper time for new beginnings. The calendar gives these dates for five different world religions: Islam, Judaism, Christianity, Buddhism and Hinduism, as well as the Chinese State calendar. Let's make the honouring of these sacred Moons of different cultures a socially cohesive force in the modern world.

Through these sacred events one can experience the concept of the dark time of New Moon as a beginning. In today's electric-light society one is hardly able to sense the significance of this time of the month when the Moon cannot be seen by day or night. Mental health, balance in life and happiness are all assisted by living more in tune with the lunar calendar.

Here are the 'sacred Moons' of 2020, i.e. the Full Moons of Easter and Wesak (Buddhist) plus other New Moon festivals.

Chinese New Year	25 January, Year of the Metal Rat	New Moon on 24 January
Hindu New Year	24 March	New Moon on 24 March
Easter Sunday	12 April	Full Moon on 8 April
Buddhist Wesak	7 May	Full Moon on 7 May
Start of Ramadan	24 April	New Moon on 23 April
Islamic New Year	20 August	New Moon on 19 August
Jewish New Year	18 September	New Moon on 17 September
Diwali	14 November	New Moon on 15 November